For David.

INDIA HICKS

ISLAND STYLE

RIZZOLI
NEW YORK

New York · Paris · London · Milan

TABLE OF CONTENTS

ABOVE: Squinting into the Bahamian sunshine, in an attractive pair of hand-me-down red shorts, with my godfather, The Prince of Wales.
OPPOSITE: Foreword by His Royal Highness The Prince of Wales.

CLARENCE HOUSE

Having known India since she was a very small baby, I was most touched she should have asked her old Godfather to write a foreword to this charming book…

Her love for the Bahamas and her passion for preserving and celebrating the unique heritage of the islands were clearly born out of her childhood associations with the islands of Windermere and Eleuthera. It was on Windermere that her parents had a rather special beach house, which I remember well from my visits nearly forty years ago when India and her brother and sister were very energetic, observant children.

The influence of her father, David Hicks, on her eye for detail and colour is only too obvious as you read through this book. So, too, is India's enduring relationship with the island life, culture and identity of the Bahamas. I can only hope that, amongst other things, this book will remind people that the outstanding beauty of these seven hundred or so islands and cays goes beyond their pink sands, clear waters and tropical flora and fauna. It lies in the harmony that exists between the natural environment and the people who inhabit it. Bahamians know only too well the value of respecting their landscape and surrounding ocean. Approximately sixty per cent of the country's income comes from tourism, and the Atlantic waters are the lifeblood of the islands' "blue economy." Without sustainable development and conservation, the future of this precious archipelago, its wildlife and its island communities would be at great risk. I very much hope that India's book will provide a way of telling this vital and enduring story…

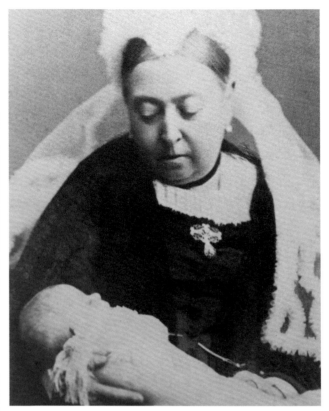

ABOVE, CLOCKWISE FROM TOP LEFT: My mother, pensive under the weight of that tiara. My grandmother, painted by Salvador Dalí. Queen Victoria, about to be boxed by my grandfather. My grandparents, ready for action. My grandmother with her lion, Sabi. My mother, in her father's jacket. They measured her growth by how it fit. My mother (right) and Mahatma Gandhi at one of his public prayer meetings, sharing the same optician?

PAST AND PRESENT

I've never had a plan. One thing just led to another. In my early school days, things looked bright. "Head girl material," read one report. But it was all downhill from there. And I had a lot to live up to.

My grandfather was the great-grandson of Queen Victoria. He claimed to have knocked the spectacles off the end of her nose as a baby when she held him. Clearly emboldened by this move, he went on to become Supreme Allied Commander, Viceroy of India, First Sea Lord, and Chief of the Defence Staff.

My bewitching grandmother Edwina Mountbatten was beautiful, vivacious, intelligent, and forthright. Who else could have returned home from a trip to Africa with several hundred photographs and a three-month-old lion cub? In all the accounts of the violent disruption that followed the partition of India, my grandmother is universally praised for her heroic efforts in relieving the misery, and she continued to lead a life of service long after her viceroyalty in India.

My mother's own childhood was an extraordinary whirlwind of English eccentricity, Hollywood glamour, and political education. She came of age in India during independence, attended prayer meetings with Mahatma Gandhi, and had a front-row seat at many a historical event. She returned to England to serve as a bridesmaid in Princess Elizabeth's wedding to Prince Philip and then as lady-in-waiting to the young princess, and was at her side, up a tree in Africa, when Princess Elizabeth learned her father had died and she was queen.

And then she married David Hicks, my father and arguably the most influential interior designer of his generation. With shops in fifteen countries throughout the world, my father designed everything around him, from the royal apartments of the Prince of Wales to the nose of a client.

I grew up in the rolling Chiltern Hills of Oxfordshire. Our home, Britwell, a charming Georgian brick house built in 1728, had two sweeping wings and an oval chapel set behind one of them. Large enough to be tricky

ABOVE: My mother and her astonishing waistline greet a young Prince Charles, as her groom, my father, laughs beside her. They married on a snowy day in Romsey Abbey, in Hampshire, in 1960. So cold and full of snow that Noël Coward said, "I know David's a decorator, but this is carrying decorating too far!" My mother's dress and snow white fur collar and cuffs were designed by Worth.

ABOVE: As a bridesmaid to Princess Diana and Prince Charles (back row, third from left). Really one of my worst hair days ever, and I was feeling very awkward in that frilly dress. Where were my jeans? Following: Britwell House. The home where I grew up during my early years and in which my mother lived quietly, as my father prepared to take the design world by storm. The monument was built forty years after the house in 1764.

ABOVE, CLOCKWISE FROM TOP LEFT: My sister (left) successfully modeling her South Seas skirt whilst I curl my toes. My parents on a casual night at home. My mother's hairstyle, designed by my father, showcased in this family photo. OPPOSITE, CLOCKWISE FROM TOP LEFT: Our dining room, originally a chapel built in 1767. My father's library, painted black with simple stainless steel shelves and an impressive lineup of telephones. My brother and sister in the nursery at Britwell. The tricycle was 1880. I don't think I ever saw Ashley ride a horse again.

FOLLOWING: My parents riding in the fields at Britwell. My father, never one for just popping on any old pair of jodhpurs, had his streamlined, and topped off by a toreador hat, somewhat surprising for the English countryside. PAGE 21: Bruce Weber captured David, me, and Barrel the day before our eldest was born. PAGE 22: Kitty Soft Paws plans an attack on an unsuspecting lizard in the warm evening sun. It's a rare moment that there are no children fighting in the pool beyond. PAGES 26–27: David and me and our horde of children, seemingly behaving on the garden steps. Left to right: Felix, Amory, Domino, Conrad, and Wesley.

when house-training a puppy—so many bedrooms in which to pee without ever being caught. The house was surrounded by 578 acres across which I would ride, bareback and wild.

Up till that point, no one had had either the guts or the inclination to decorate a home any other way than the dusty, predictable, flowery chintz of a traditional English country house. My father was to change all that.

With Britwell as his showroom and laboratory, he turned decorating on its head, mixing old with new, electrifying color schemes, and making bold geometric statements. As David Hicks set the design world alight, my mother retreated into the background, happy with her horses, dogs, books, and privacy.

As children, my brother, sister, and I spent most of our time in the nursery, a world of its own run by nannies—starched at first and gradually over the years not so starched—with the required wooden, velvet-seated rocking horse and slightly less child-friendly 1880 French tricycle, but most memorably a swing harnessed to the ceiling at the end of the lengthy nursery passageway.

Before long we were sent to boarding school, which is not nearly as Dickensian as it may sound. In fact Gordonstoun, an unusual school set challengingly in the north of freezing Scotland, where my godfather, the Prince of Wales, also went, provided me not perhaps with the education my parents might have hoped for, but certainly with some lifelong memories.

Not quite knowing what to do with myself after school, I went around the world for a year with a backpack, a cousin, and not much money. I returned to England to find my father had compiled a list of dukes he thought I should marry. Each time one of the dukes married someone other than my sister or me, that duke was scratched off the list. The list got shorter, the dukes more dodgy, so I ran off to Boston with a Greek boyfriend and took a degree in photography, fell onto the other side of the camera, and wandered around the world again, this time as a model.

Trying to find a little peace after a crisis with my sister, I retreated to the house my parents built in the Bahamas. After several dark days alone, I found my way to neighboring Harbour Island. I had been reminded that an old friend was now living in this remote spot. As the island is only half a mile wide and three long, it did not take much detective work to find David. Shoeless and suntanned, he was running a small hotel

with a copy of Joseph Conrad's *An Outcast of the Islands* in one hand and a Bloody Mary in the other. Four months later I was pregnant.

We bought Hibiscus Hill virtually unseen. The real estate agent looked at me—unmarried, barefoot, and pregnant—disapprovingly. She would not let us into the house to view it. I peered through the windows. David toured the gardens. We both agreed it felt like home.

We never married. We didn't feel the need. Somehow being strangers in a strange land bonded us more than any ceremony ever could. And Hibiscus Hill provided us with the blank canvas upon which we could paint our own story.

It took many years before I dared to call myself a designer. Being the daughter of David Hicks, and the sister of Ashley, cast quite a shadow. But living so far away and with my own David now firmly holding my hand, I felt a new chapter opening up.

As the months rolled into years, David and I began to understand that our island life and decorating sensibility were a combination of our traditional British past and our richly flavored Caribbean present, all mixed up with our own eccentricities.

As I write this book I am thankful—for my past and my present. When I think of my island life, I imagine I am running on the pink sand beach at sunrise with my dogs, my children safe and my house quiet. While I run, the small town across the dunes behind me stirs beneath a blanket of breaking dawn. I can hear the faint cry of the cockerels strutting along the lanes; the smell of the salt air and casuarina trees floats down to the water's edge, and I am struck by the splendor of sea, land, and sky. The architecture and the view from the harbor has hardly changed in the last 200 years, although the many layers of time are faintly visible. The churches and historic wooden cottages echo the memories of many generations and the rhythms of island life.

But the idea that this small island should never change is ridiculous. It has been slowly changing for centuries and will go on changing far into the future. We can only hope that as we move forward we remember, and prize, the simple things island life has to offer—for ourselves, for our children, and for their children.

There is so much to be lost in forgetting and so much to be gained in preserving this island heritage.

MAROONED

Plenty has been written about the history and people of Harbour Island and Eleuthera, from the Arawaks and Lucayans who arrived some 2,000 years ago to the Eleutherian Adventurers, an effete bunch of British malcontents shipwrecked off the Devil's Backbone and forced to survive in what is now known as Preacher's Cave.

The islands had a history of turmoil pretty much from the get-go, with Spanish, British, and American rebels snatching ownership throughout the next century, not to mention the merry bands of pirates and buccaneers who decided to focus their activities on the Out Islands of the Bahamas. There were more pirates than civilians living in Nassau at the turn of the seventeenth century. We still have a few swashbucklers hanging around today.

There is a great amount of snobbism involved when talking about Harbour Island (anyone who refers to it simply as "Harbour" has immediately and unwittingly revealed himself as a tourist). You will often overhear winter residents competing about how long they have been visiting the island. I was three years old when I first made the trip across the bay from the neighboring island of Windermere, where we holidayed every year as one large family, a group that often would include a certain godfather. Enticed into the car with the promise of ice cream, my parents insisted my brother, sister, and I make the stuffy drive north with them, past the sleepy Eleuthera settlements to Three Island Dock to be ferried across to Harbour Island, known then, and now, as the jewel in the crown.

Twenty-five years after that initial visit, I made Harbour Island my home.

Harbour Island is everything the Bahamas should be: a small community of people who say good morning and good night to one another amongst frangipani and palm trees, pretty timber houses painted bright gelato colors, white picket fences, crystal clear waters, and exquisite pink sand beaches.

Moving from a somewhat faster-paced life in New York City to this speck in the Caribbean Sea certainly proved challenging. It's one thing to go to an island on holiday. It's quite another to live there. Three months

of hurricane season and a goods boat that often doesn't reach. Power outages for endless stretches of time, and one doctor shared between several communities. The island is proud of its fire engine, but no one knows where the keys are.

Hibiscus Hill became my life raft as I adjusted to island life.

Pootling through our stone gates and up our winding driveway, you will find our home at the top of a rise overlooking town, sitting proudly amongst a jungle of palm trees, the bay to the west, the ocean to the east, and the sound of the waves rhythmically breaking on the three-mile pink sand beach at the bottom of the garden.

Hibiscus Hill came fully furnished, with salmon chintz cushions on shell-shaped sofas, an immaculate heavy-glassed dining table, an alarming ornate chandelier, thick bedroom carpets (confusing for a house in the tropics), and trinkets in every corner. We hardly knew where to begin.

What we did know was that we wanted our home to feel more 1850 than 1950. So we began by removing the white tiled floor, at which point the inherited housekeeper left, disgusted.

In place of the tiles, we laid unusually large planks of fir that reached a full sixteen feet long. We stained them a dark shade of oak, but over the years traffic from family and friends and the relentless blaze of the Bahamian sun have given them a warmer, lighter look. As paint was readily available (unlike toothpaste or face cream), we decided to experiment. The sitting room and dining room went from a Palm Beach white to Mediterranean rust, but once we lived with that for a few weeks we realized we'd been mad to choose it. We were living in the tropics, not on the Côte d'Azur. So rust was out, replaced with the palest gray. David now claims all these changes came about because I was pregnant, and a pregnant woman should never be left alone with a Pantone paint deck. Unfortunately for him, I became pregnant another three times. Our walls have suffered.

Of course the entrance of a house is really just about that, making an entrance. To our dismay, the first thing you saw was a rather nasty wooden console that we acquired with the house. We painted it white, hoping for the best. Now, years later, with too many children and the demands of daily life, the table remains there, as hideous as ever. We all know you should live in a house for a while before making design decisions, but this is perhaps taking it too far.

PAGE 28: There is a captivating drama when you set eyes on Harbour Island bay, bordered by beaches and guided by the rhythms of the sea, and, of course, boasting that absurd color palette. PAGE 30: Every morning when the sun is just breaking through the palm trees and I take the dogs for their morning pee, I look back up our driveway and feel blessed. PAGE 31: David and I bought a pair of stone dogs at a flea market in Nashville. How improbable is that? We shipped them home and placed them on our gateposts to guard our entrance. PAGES 32–33: When we first moved into Hibiscus Hill, we removed all the hibiscus. We simply wanted a green garden. Green on green on green. Except, of course, the pink oleander. That was allowed to stay—a jolt of tropical color in an otherwise clean palette. PAGE 35: We inherited this fireplace with the house. Rather too ornate for our tastes, but used surprisingly often. On top stands one of our trademark palm-frond displays. OPPOSITE: Our dining table and chairs discovered in New Orleans many moons ago. Unfortunately, the ravenous termites seem to enjoy them as much as we do. ABOVE: This table was designed by us and made locally, which is charmingly apparent. A collection of unrelated objects sits on top—everything from a wooden toy car to my grandmother's pigskin writing case.

PAGES 38–39: The archway between our sitting room and dining room highlights the unusually wide fir floorboards we laid down, up to sixteen feet long in some cases, and houses our lending library of straw hats. ABOVE: My prized collection of lucky nuts (left), each discovered on the beach during my early morning runs over the past two decades, and our bowl of stolen cricket balls (right), a constant reminder of our other home. OPPOSITE: A scrap of material from one of my father's many exotic travels, which I made into a cushion. FOLLOWING: Another piece of slightly suspicious furniture that we never got around to changing. Painted white in an effort to disguise it more, it at least serves the purpose of displaying good Georgian presentation bowls, blue-and-white china, and a welcoming shark's jaw.

Most entryways serve the serious purpose of providing somewhere to lay your hat, fling your keys, and toss the mail. Our house didn't come with keys, so we have never locked a door, the Bahamian postal service feels no particular urgency regarding the delivery of mail, and our hats, oddly, lie on our library shelves.

Our entryway, however, is like the opening line of our autobiography, filled as it is with Georgian silver bowls that belonged to my great-grandfather, blue-and-white china, gifts from David's relatives, and one of the black hibiscus candles I developed, which has a scent with the power to evoke Harbour Island.

At the foot of the console is a ceramic bowl laden with slightly tattered cricket balls. They were once upon a time inadvertently whacked into the garden of my mother's housekeeper in England. Annoyed by their appearance, she would refuse to return them to the local cricket club, whose grounds were located just beyond her garden wall.

We dress both this hall table and the space above the sitting room fireplace with oversized palm fronds. Tropical flowers don't last long after they have been cut, but the green fronds can last several weeks and are, thankfully, not in short supply. This gesture has become somewhat of a trademark. We bring vast vases of palm fronds into all our rooms, and even my shop now feels somewhat naked without them.

Tory Burch came for a drink one evening. I am a huge admirer of hers, as she is of my father. She looked around our sitting room and said how nice it was to see a home so "under-decorated." David and I decided we were going to take that as a compliment, and we began to explore the idea of under-decorating.

However, the most challenging part of telling our own story was negotiating our individual tastes. Having been brought up under the imposing eye of my famous father, I had strong opinions, and David certainly cared about decorating details and was passionately invested in the island's traditional architecture. Stormy debates were par for the course. One thing we did agree on was that when decorating in the tropics, neither David nor I were ever drawn to slick materials, flashy fabrics, or overengineered designs. We always opt for those that more fittingly express the spirit of the place, the atmosphere of island life, captured by the faint suggestion of sand and seaweed, piles of well-thumbed books, simple dreams, and the consistent echo of our English past, stumbling from one world to another.

ABOVE: Harbour Island can show off eight or nine different churches, which is impressive considering the island is only three miles long and half a mile wide. Of course, the fact that you can buy a beer in at least forty places is even more impressive. This church happens to be on Eleuthera. OPPOSITE: Built in 1768, St. John's Anglican Church is where we attend midnight mass at 10:00 P.M. on Christmas Eve. Yes, 10:00 P.M. It's also where my dear British friend Ms. Elodie Ling met with God every Sunday, and where we bid farewell to Wesley's Bahamian mother on a warm spring day that neither he nor I will ever forget.

Saint John's
Anglican
Church
EST. 1768

OPPOSITE AND ABOVE: I grew up traveling the Queen's Highway, my father pointing out the historic Haynes Library as we passed through Governor's Harbour, a place not only proud of its library, but also home to the only traffic light on the 110 miles of Eleuthera. FOLLOWING: Apart from the air-conditioning unit on the side of this church, little must have changed in this view over the past 200 years. It is painted in the generic Nassau pink, similar to the inside of a mature conch shell.

HIBISCUS HILL
ARBOUR ISLAND
THE BAHAMAS
WEST INDIES

INHERITANCE

I have inherited a few bits here and there for which I am very grateful. My great-grandfather's giltwood console table, for instance, circa 1730, with a serpentine Portor marble top above a pierced patera and foliate-carved frieze, ogee legs with satyr-mask headers and pied-de-biche, and a shell-carved stretcher. (And yes, I am as lost as you are with that description.) It's quite an intimidating piece of furniture, and I can never really find the right location for it. To make matters even more complicated, I can't sell it because my mother would kill me.

One of the other things I have inherited is an obsessive desire for collecting, organizing, and tablescaping. *Tablescape.* My father invented this term, or so he claimed. My brother, Ashley, would know for sure.

No matter whether he did or did not, he was the master of it. As long as I can remember, I have lived in rooms whose surfaces are filled with collections of objects. And as my father illustrated, these can be ancient or barely even antique, or, as in our case, inexpensive mixed with very inexpensive, simply organized by color and characteristic David Hicks precision.

Recently I was sent in the post a 1967 issue of *House Beautiful* magazine. Starring on the cover was a table from my mother's boudoir, captioned "David Hicks's tablescape, Oxfordshire." On the table were a few objects perfectly positioned, which over the years had been added to or slightly rearranged. Never by my mother, in whose room the table was located, but always by my father. Studying the magazine cover so many years later, memories of that nearly forgotten world came back—a world of butlers and chauffeurs and children who were rarely seen and certainly never heard. One of the opaque smoky green glass boxes displayed on that tabletop caught my eye, and I remembered that my mother kept the Good Boy Choc Drops she would feed her miniature dachshund at teatime in it. I also remembered that I would steal into that room and furtively open the box and eat the doggie chocolate drops myself. Dear God, I hope my daughter, Domino, is not eating Banger's treats.

When I bought my first apartment in London, my father, of course, had a heavy hand in guiding its decoration. A tented bed, in David Hicks fabric, complete with matching bedcover, cushions, and vanity chair. The sitting room also strictly David Hicks: geometrics, old and new furniture, and, of course, the inevitable tablescapes.

Upon arriving in New York to live and work as a model, an ocean away from my family, I thought, "Right, bloody decorative freedom," and on my paltry student budget off I went to the flea market.

Once finished, I stood back to admire my freshly decorated home and was astonished to find a David Hicks–inspired loft before my eyes. Fire-engine-red walls, geometric rugs, Louis XV fauteuils, and, yes, side tables and desktops with disparate and somewhat eclectic groups of objects, all certainly valueless in every aspect, other than the fact they screamed "You can't escape!" at me.

Now, after many years of decorating my own homes or snooping around the homes of others, I realize the enormous effort it takes to put those finishing touches on a newly completed project. Simply choosing which door handles to buy can be overwhelming enough, let alone deciding on the shape of a sofa or color of the walls. But the final little details are, in my opinion, what makes a house a home, and that includes the tablescapes. So even if you don't happen to own a lump of quartz from the Sahara or a collection of porphyry or a mass of rock crystal objects, don't panic. You will find a starting point in something. Even if it's an old wooden photo frame, go out and buy two more inexpensive frames of a similar nature, place some black-and-white photos in them, and put the three frames together. Next to them maybe place a leather box, on top of which you could add a lump of coral, and beside which you might place the bone-handled hairbrushes from your childhood and your grandfather's travel clock that no longer works but looks handsome in the mix. An empty jam jar with a single rose and a pretty bottle of fragrance now complete the scene. Perfect in your bedroom on a chest of drawers.

In the living room, you might want to be a bit more bold and unconventional. The coffee table could start with a pile of picture books, topped off with a china dish filled with bead necklaces, perhaps a smelly candle and a backgammon set and an oversized conch shell brought back from your holiday to Harbour Island. A table in our sitting room is crowded with a collection of boxes and objects in similar shapes and sizes, an antique watercolor case given to my eldest as a christening present, my grandmother's pigskin writing case, a box of dominos, and an indestructible wooden toy car—the interest between all these simply being color and texture.

Your home now has that extra layer of attention, even if David Hicks wasn't your dad.

PAGE 50: The beetle is a welcome visitor in our Bahamian home. This gentle creature has brought me much luck: five children and a home filled with happiness. Don't panic, he doesn't always bring five children. PAGE 53: A fresh wild spider lily sits near the fragrance she inspired and beside my grandmother's shagreen powder case, the livery buttons from my grandfather's household, my father's iconic *H* symbol, and my mother's charm bracelet. OPPOSITE: The Hibiscus Hill bar, well stocked with local limes, sea grape leaf, and the requisite island machete, which inexplicably seems to lurk on the chopping board. Above: Our kitchen table is hardly ever naked. Once the cereal boxes have been cleared away, I can't resist a little fruit tablescape. An inherited disease.

ABOVE: Making order out of chaos: color-coding books, amassing objects of similar texture and tone, layering life and memories into tablescapes. OPPOSITE: Each of those little silver cases on my bedside table holds one of my children's teeth. It's a bit creepy, but surely you are not meant to throw them out? PAGE 58: A rose from Princess Diana's wedding bouquet (she had one set in glass as a gift to each of her bridesmaids) beside a Rajputana dagger handle, soapstone beetles, a jade elephant, and a box of matches, for no particular reason. PAGE 59: A collection of shagreen objects on my bedroom desk, inherited from my grandmother. When I open the powder compact, I can smell 1930. With a large amount of determination and paint thinner, we stripped back the original paint finish to reveal the desk's bare bones.

L·O·V·E
Harbour Island, June 2011

D. L. & Co
MODERN ALCHEMISTS
AND
PURVEYORS OF CURIOUS GOODS

OPPOSITE: There were more pirates than civilians living on Harbour Island at the turn of the eighteenth century, so that may explain my fascination with skulls, especially a tablescape of them. ABOVE LEFT: David's bar at King's Treat organized into a tablescape overseen by Tintin. ABOVE RIGHT: Books, books, paintings, and paintings, plus three plastic fish under Perspex and an obscure green candle, masquerading as a shell, fill this corner table.

ABOVE: The table that holds our household batteries in a drawer is romanticized by random objects unified by color and my childhood gardening panier, now brimming with lucky nuts. OPPOSITE: David's past and present: Bahamian dollars, British passport, and a handful of cuff links.

OPPOSITE: Red glass coral, as fragile as the real thing, on top of an irresistible eighteenth-century watercolor set. Every time a child is tempted to paint with this, we scream "Nnnnnnoooo!" ABOVE LEFT: In true David Hicks tablescaping style, here is a collection of utterly random objects held together by color only. ABOVE RIGHT: Wooden Venetian puzzles sit below pencil golf, a pencil-and-paper game my grandfather invented for his two daughters.

ABOVE LEFT: We attempt to decorate using natural textures and organic shapes, although I am not at all sure how natural blue coral is. But you have to admire the shell-shaped mantel. ABOVE RIGHT: These two colossal shells were certainly not found on our beach. OPPOSITE: Repurposing a shot glass into a vase is ideal until the party gets going.

CHAOS

Our kitchen is the command-and-control headquarters of Hibiscus Hill, center of all chaos and the place where we congregate. I can't cook, but I can direct, much to the annoyance of Claire, known as Top Banana, who does cook. Top Banana came from England for a few weeks to help out after the birth of my third son and stayed for ten years, married a Bahamian, and lives at No. 1 Chick Farm. Anyone crossing our kitchen doorstep will be greeted by the impressive sight of Top Banana, oven mitts in hand; typically she is swatting a child away from the larder door. *No, you cannot have a snack as it's nearly lunchtime.*

My other boss is Marissa, affectionately rechristened Rissy by my children. Rissy is in charge of the house and, of course, island gossip; all insider intelligence comes from Rissy. She has held this strategic position for more than fifteen years.

From the heart of our home comes the feeding of the 5,000. During the holidays there is a steady stream of bodies around our kitchen table, testing the patience of Top Banana and Rissy. The table was designed by me many years ago and has the original stainless steel, which has been scrubbed so often it's taken on an entirely new patina. The table is normally creaking with titanic-sized bowls of tropical fruit, not just because we try to persuade our children that fruit tastes nearly as good as chocolate, but because we love the way fruit looks—inviting and decoratively fab.

My mother, a beloved and much welcomed guest in our home who joins us for the month of December, is of a generation and upbringing who never had the need to enter the kitchen and always took breakfast in bed (admittedly a step forward from the Russian princess who, upon deciding she needed to run away from home, reached the palace front door and had no idea how to open it). Breakfast in bed is now a well-documented art in our household: the tray needs to have folding legs, because you can't possibly balance a tray without legs safely on your lap, although we are allowed to overlook the newspaper slot, as the island newspapers are inevitably a few days out of date. The teapot needs to have been warmed through *before* the hot water is added (she can tell when you skip this step), two bags, one for the pot and one for you, tea leaves are fine but must be accompanied by requisite strainer, and milk, cold, in a matching jug and *never in first*, which conflicts with general opinion. A full breakfast follows, always in stages: fresh orange juice, then eggs and bacon, and finally a toasted English muffin, in a toast rack (otherwise it goes soft, obviously) and enjoyed with honey, brought out from England.

My mother has spent seventeen Christmases with us. That makes seventeen very traditional English Christmases spent under swaying palm trees, ten of which have been cooked by Top Banana and all of which have featured Christmas crackers from Fortnum & Mason and a Christmas pudding from Tesco. (Apparently The Queen buys hers there, too.)

Other holidays deserve their own celebrations. We have hosted many a Halloween party for our small community school, each year becoming more ghoulish, until the time a rather mad island friend dressed improbably in a yellow oilskin and a Hannibal Lecter mask broke down the garden gate and ran around the garden swinging a working chainsaw. Most of the children left in tears. After that we dialed back a little.

More successfully, we invite all of the school to our yearly Easter egg hunt. We serve the parents cold Pimm's with fresh cucumber and mint as the children dash about, crazed on chocolate and out of their minds with excitement over the fact that the Hibiscus Hill Easter bunny bounced all over the garden again.

We have invented every sort of birthday party theme possible, from camouflaged army to pink marshmallows. When it was time for our fourth son's eighth birthday, exhausted of ideas, a food fight was suggested and promptly arranged. Down to the beach we went, paper plates piled high with wet spaghetti, whipped cream, and vats of jelly. The children lined up in order of size, someone blew a whistle, and all hell broke loose. The air filled with food being flung. Children ran in delighted terror as even parents began to join in, tossing and smearing their way through the crowd of bodies, after which we all washed off in the cool turquoise ocean. Now, please don't lecture me about this: my children are very aware that throwing food around is not acceptable and that others in different parts of the world are not fortunate enough to have food at all. This was a one-off occasion on a sunny birthday afternoon.

As the children grow up, so do our ideas. For one of the teenage boys, we celebrated with a considerable fire pit, burrowed out by the water's edge, and we sat around it toasting marshmallows as the sun set.

PAGE 68: A cluster of coconuts, a pyramid of oranges, or, as here, a branch of bananas—we will use any tropical fruit to add life to a tabletop, and gathering it gives our children license to wield that machete. PAGE 71: I grew up with peacocks. My father felt they improved the outside of the house. They did keep us awake at night, however. Princess Elizabeth of Yugoslavia once asked the housekeeper to shut them up when she was staying. Our five small lovebirds are no competition. OPPOSITE: Laying the table for our very traditional English Christmas. In the tropics. ABOVE: And to dispel any question about reindeer existing in the Bahamas, here, top left, is one to prove it. Our table is a juxtaposition of British Christmas crackers and tropical starfish.

ABOVE: With five children, we have explored just about every birthday party theme imaginable, some with more success than others, but stringing up those marshmallows (left) was hell. OPPOSITE: Halloween is taken seriously on Harbour Island. One year, Wesley was stuffed into a coffin as we trick-or-treated around town. Neither he, nor I, will ever forget or forgive that experience. FOLLOWING: Now that our children are more acceptable we include them in all dinners, which means our table regularly extends from one end of the terrace to the other. We gave up renting chairs from the church and submitted to buying our own folding ones.

We lit lanterns and released them into the glowing pink sky, wishing him health and happiness, although really we should have been praying for my sanity. How was I going to cope with four teenage boys?

The trickiest event we ever handled was Top Banana's wedding dinner. Tricky, of course, because if Top Banana was getting ready for her wedding, who was cooking for the 100 guests? Helpful, confident hands came to the rescue in the kitchen, and Linda, my partner in crime at our Sugar Mill boutique, worked with me to set the scene on our terrace. White paper lanterns floated on fishing line above tables borrowed from the church, while hundreds of white balloons filled our pool, hibiscus flowers drifted in champagne, a buffet table heaved with choice, and a lavish mound of homemade profiteroles, alight with sparklers, was presented to the bride and groom. Top Banana's Bahamian father-in-law stood up, swaying somewhat from side to side. He told the silenced crowd that he was proud of his son, as he was of all his other 24 children, but that was it, he said, no more children for him, 25 was enough. He returned to Nassau and later that year became the father of twins.

I always enjoy our parties. I have fun setting the tables in various ways, moving location, and thinking up new decorations, whether it's a table sprinkled with lucky nuts we have collected from the beach, or Eiffel Tower–sized vases with palm fronds, or a simple assortment of shells mixed with votive candles. I change the tablecloth from formal white to a stretch of colored linen fabric left over from reupholstering bedroom chairs, or possibly an Indian mirrored bedspread. I mix up the location and the guests as much as I mix up the decoration. And David mixes up the drinks.

Most evenings during the holidays, though, we sit as a family around our terrace dining table under a canopy of stars, with the smell of sea air and night-blooming jasmine. David, the children, and I gently argue the more important issues of life, like whether your eyes really turn square if you watch too much TV, while an uninvited gecko tiptoes past on the warm ground. A lot of life happens around our dining table that holds many family secrets, and underneath which lies a snoozing dog. Or two. It's hard to imagine Hibiscus Hill without the chaos.

PAGE 78: I can't resist a white tablecloth, candles, and flowers. Thank God Top Banana tied the knot so I finally had the chance to justify this. PAGES 80–81 Frangipani in sherry glasses and a mass of shells, stones, and votive candles fill the table. ABOVE LEFT: The DRINKS MONITOR badge seems shamelessly redundant. ABOVE RIGHT: My father abhorred ice from a common ice machine. How lucky, then, that ours never worked and to this day we fill the trays by hand. OPPOSITE: Olympia kicks off cocktail hour. FOLLOWING: Beware of paper lanterns and heavy evening dew. They don't agree with each other.

ABOVE: Even for a Virgo, this fire pit came close to perfection. To create it, David had three pairs of hands, two broom handles, one long piece of rope, and several shovels. He found a center spot and planted the broom handle. Tied one end of the rope to the broom handle, tied the other end to the second broom handle. Walked around in a wide circle tracing in the sand as he went. And then dug.

ABOVE: I change the china as often as I change the table setting and decoration. The pink set, vaguely seen here, has hand-painted collections of nautilus shells on it. You'll have to take my word for it. FOLLOWING: Birthday cake, balloons, and a good sunset. Oh, yes, and a pod of baby dolphins swimming by (sadly neither the cake nor the dolphins are visible here). It certainly makes up for the three months of hurricane season.

PINK SAND

Yes, it really is pink. There's a very thought-through scientific reason for this, but the short version is that it has something to do with the finely pulverized remains of calcium carbonate shells and skeletons of invertebrates and something else to do with the unpronounceable foraminifera, which are dark red skeletal animals that grow profusely on the underside of the coral reefs. When the red forms die, the skeletons plummet to the ocean floor and the wave action erodes them into...well, pink sand.

Mother Nature had some fun designing the Bahamas. Just spend time under the water, as I did during those first unhurried years, and you'll be treated to an array of visual delights: the green moray, the red snapper, the yellow goatfish, the blue tang. On land there are the rock iguana and his splendid red neck, curly-tailed lizards, dwarf geckos, fat-headed frogs, money moths, grass snakes, swimming pigs, and all the exotic birds listed in James Bond's book *Birds of the West Indies*. However, could Mother Nature not have stopped before the no-see-um? I don't think we need that smaller, more irritating relation to the mosquito.

Color and pattern are present everywhere here and quickly influenced many of my own designs for bedding, jewelry, and beauty products. The flora and fauna are equally brilliant: flame trees, frangipani, hibiscus, oleander, and the courageous spider lily, who grows improbably out of the pink sand. Her intoxicating scent became the foundation for two of my fragrance projects.

I have always admired the pattern of the palm tree, both her leaves and her trunk. A tree we take for granted, but brilliantly designed to bend, rather than snap, in hurricane-force winds. My children were always amazed to discover that in other parts of the world trees lost their leaves. How odd, they thought, as odd as

PAGE 90: The sun continues to rise and set, the hurricanes continue to ravage, and our sand remains uniquely pink on the beaches of tiny Harbour Island. ABOVE: Continuously inspired by Mother Nature, I steal many of her ideas when designing my own collections and interiors. OPPOSITE: Most self-respecting old homes in the West Indies hold a copy of James Bond's book. Ian Fleming spotted this whilst looking for a name for the hero of his spy novel. FOLLOWING: In those first uncomplicated years of living in the Bahamas, I would spend more time under the water than above, always enjoying an astounding feast for the eyes.

Birds
of the
West
Indies

James
Bond

Second
Edition

G

HOUGHTON
MIFFLIN
COMPANY

winter clothes. One holiday in England, I discovered they had removed all their clothes in the back of the car and were happily being driven through the London traffic in their birthday suits.

With Mother Nature's infinite combinations, there are no preconceived notions or fears about what goes with what. David Hicks and Mother Nature both believed there was no such thing as a clashing color.

Color, clashing or otherwise, is seen not only in nature but also in much of the architecture here. Throughout the West Indies, most of the houses are painted dazzling colors. Between the two World Wars, paint became a common imported item, and bright colors soon replaced the natural hues of the raw materials. Every change of surface from doorframes to window shutters became an opportunity for color. The government buildings, the post office, and the library are all painted conch pink—even our prisons are conch pink.

With the kaleidoscope of color on the outside, we wanted a quieter palette on the inside. Soft almond, dusty coral, muted clay, dove gray. And then we couldn't resist: we painted our staircase hot fuchsia. So successful is this that many a designer passing through our home asks what the color is. We hardly dare to confess it was actually a mistake. The local paint store ran out of one base and swapped it with another, and no one now remembers which.

But for the most part we keep stronger colors to just the odd pop: the exuberantly hued skull towels hanging in our slightly scruffy downstairs bathroom, the scarlet sofa in our sitting room, the red chairs in the kitchen, a vibrantly patterned pillow on an otherwise unremarkable chair, the fluorescent painted bicycle signposting the Sugar Mill boutique. And when I glance inside my wardrobe, I see the same principle at work—a subtle palette with the odd burst of color.

At Christmastime, this island goes bananas with color during the festival of Junkanoo. This word must be said in a hushed Holy Grail kind of way. Junkanoo defines the culture of the Bahamas and commands the attention and attendance of most Bahamians. It is believed that this festival began during the sixteenth and

PAGE 97: Our staircase, painted a watermelon pink that we never managed to re-create again, and an unremarkable birdcage, made remarkable when filled with tiny lovebirds who escape regularly. OPPOSITE: It's quite an exercise to train the children to hang up their wet swimming towels, but it's even harder to train them to hang them with the skulls facing top and out. ABOVE: The pineapple, a common symbol of welcome in the tropics, is seen throughout our tiny island in many guises. Another successful design from Mother Nature. We pass this fence daily on the school run; I hope my children never forget their tropical commute.

ABOVE AND OPPOSITE: For the most part, Dunmore Town is made up of lovely warm materials and colors, richly patterned picket fences, shutters that shield a stranger's stare, and verandas that shade stray dogs. Tiny cottages perch next to one another in a visual richness and architectural rhythm.

FOLLOWING: A broken-down old bike, about to be tossed, was repainted by my children. Festooned with a bunch of plastic flowers from the funeral parlor, it now boldly signposts the Sugar Mill shop. Which is certainly an improvement from the bra that we once extravagantly hung as a window treatment.

seventeenth centuries. The slaves were given a special holiday when they could leave the plantations to be with their families. They celebrated with African dance, music, and costumes.

The origin of the word is obscure. Some say it comes from the French *l'inconnu* (meaning the unknown), in reference to the masks worn by the dancers; others relate it to the name John Canoe, an African tribal chief who demanded the right to celebrate with his people even after being brought to the West Indies in slavery.

Every year each Junkanoo troupe selects a theme for its costumes, and members are dressed in variations on that theme. We are Zulus because we happen to live close to Zulu headquarters, otherwise known as the Shack. Junkanoo allegiances are geographical; I'm not sure what happens if you move to a different part of the island. Inside the Shack, bands of Zulus expend astonishing amounts of artistic energy from about the middle of the year to the last moments on Christmas Day. And astonishing amounts of good old Kalik beer are drunk. The name of this beer derives from the sound of the cowbell being rung during the parade: k-k-kalik, k-k-kalik, k-k-kaliking. Of course, up on the hill the Barracks Hill Warriors are also designing and constructing costumes and huge mobile sculptures made from cardboard boxes, all covered in finely fringed, brightly colored crepe paper. But we, as Zulus, would not be welcome up the hill. On Boxing Day and New Year's Day, my children go out and "rush" with the Zulus. Not every mother gets to see her teenage boys dressed confidently in cardboard skirts they have created, during days of backbreaking cutting and pasting. And however many years you are involved with Junkanoo, you never get used to burning off bits of your skin with a glue gun.

Although this is a very good time of year for cardboard boxes, it is a bad time of year for goats. Goatskin drums are warmed by a fire. The drummers then line up with the costumed dancers, trumpeters, cowbell ringers, conch-shell blowers, and dudes with whistles. Everyone is on the street; everyone is taken up.

An explosion of color parades down Bay Street beside the charming colored cottages, just across from the pink sand beach. This ancient tradition still plays a huge part in the island's modern life.

ABOVE: Why on earth is there suddenly a picture of my wardrobe in this book? It's to demonstrate some weird notion I have about bursts of color—in the way I decorate and the way I dress. OPPOSITE: Bursts of color are found elsewhere on the island, not just inside my wardrobe.

OPPOSITE AND ABOVE: There can be no better example of an eruption of color than a Bahamian Junkanoo parade. Competition is fierce between competing troupes, and costume designs are a closely guarded secret until they are finally unveiled. A lot of glue, glitter, goatskin, and Kalik beer is involved in the weeks leading up to this.

INSIDE OUT

It's 6:30 A.M. and my daughter, Domino, has just come into my room, where I am trying to sleep. In her small arms are vast bundles of clothes. She walks out onto our bedroom veranda and hurls the clothes off. "What are you doing?" I ask sleepily. "I'm getting these out, in case there is a fire." And with that she strides off again.

I suppose that is one purpose for an upstairs veranda. The other is that this particular veranda provides a tiny oasis for David and me, every once in a while, to escape from the madding crowd. When we moved into the house, the weather-worn wrought-iron sun chairs were firmly situated on that terrace. The cushions were bursting open due to corroded zippers that no longer worked, and the backs of our legs would stick hotly to the plastic covers. We knew they had to go. But somehow life got in the way.

The view from this terrace leads through an avenue of palm trees, home-grown from coconuts planted by David in our early years at Hibiscus Hill. The bay beyond is largely obscured by the now mature trees, but the avenue makes for a handsome entrance when you arrive at the end of our driveway. That driveway has been lovingly named by David the "Avenue of the Indias," and it romantically competes with the obelisk David also created for me, although the first attempt resulted in half a ton of quick-drying cement on our terrace.

Veranda, terrace, and porch: all are hugely prominent in island life. Built around a central structure, they provide a respite from the tropical sun and protect against warm rains and trade winds.

When I first met David, on the tiny island where we now live, he was managing a small hotel and living above a tearoom in the heart of the historic town. The apartment had a shallow, gently sloping veranda, and we would sit on it silently in the early evening after he had finished work, digesting the day. We would inadvertently listen to the comings and goings in the street below and overhear all sorts of local *sip sip* (gossip). I familiarized myself with many an infamous island character from that veranda.

The year I was born, my father built an alarmingly modern beach house, Savannah, on the neighboring island of Windermere. The house was inspired by the Egyptian temple of King Zoser. The walls, inside and out,

were rendered from rough cement and the pink sand of the beach. The interior was decorated very simply: bedside tables, also made from cement, Hicks fabrics in soft pastels on heavy rough linen, a living room dominated by abstract art, and bathroom ceilings that appeared to be floating. Once the house was completed, my father began to travel the sleepy settlements of Eleuthera in search of a fading colonial Bahamas. He visited derelict houses, crumbling cottages, and wooden shacks—melancholy monuments to former life and luxury. From grand plantation houses to modest wooden dwellings, these homes shared the charm of West Indian décor—lively with character, color, and ornamental detail, and graced with verandas, terraces, and porches.

My father would retrieve balustrades from the porches and verandas of these forgotten homes, and he began to display them on the clean walls of Savannah's dining room, mixing starkly contrasting old and new in his trademark style. All this, of course, was before he decided sand was too troublesome. It got into everything. Realizing that, he never returned to the house he had built from sand.

Now Mrs. Friederich, the elderly chic Swiss lady from whom we bought Hibiscus Hill, had maintained a rigorous standard of shiny tile and peach chintz. Not a collapsing balustrade in sight. (We've always felt certain the long departed Mr. Friederich was buried somewhere under the main terrace.) However, we wanted to add in a bit of grit to this gleaming canvas—a little bit of old Bahamas. And we knew just where to begin.

Drawing inspiration from that collection on the wall of Savannah, David mapped out a design that our local carpenter could copy. Since the carpenter was on a bit of a drunk at the time, the hand-carved balustrades certainly carried a modicum more imagination than we had anticipated, but they did serve to add character to the house.

Like many traditional Caribbean homes, Hibiscus Hill sprouted additional rooms—and verandas—as our family grew. There was no grand scheme. New rooms just seemed to evolve as children arrived and as our piggy bank waxed and waned—an inadvertent warren of rooms and verandas.

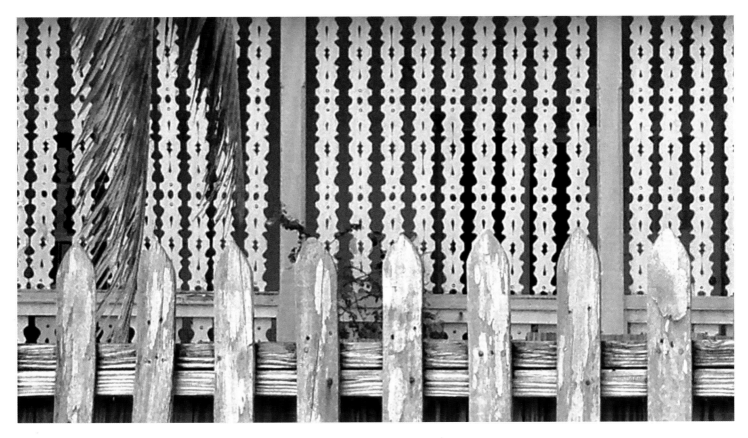

PAGE 108: Our bedroom terrace, an oasis of calm, although we never got around to changing out those hot plastic cushions that stick to our backs and legs. PAGES 110–111: The guesthouse terrace with views of both the bay and the ocean, and our most frequently chosen color scheme, white and dark mahogany. PAGE 113: Savannah, conceived by my father and inspired by an Egyptian mausoleum. Constructed from pink sand and rough cement. OPPOSITE: My father nicked pretty balustrades from porches and verandas of derelict houses and crumbling cottages in sleepy neighboring settlements and preserved them on the clean walls of Savannah. ABOVE: An elaborate balustrade on the porch of a home in Governor's Harbour. FOLLOWING: This is where all family arguments take place, at suppertime, jostling together around this table on our walled terrace. (Someone must have bribed that child to hold a book in his hands.)

My middle boys grew up spilling bits of Lego from their veranda, whilst the elder two, now teenagers, escape into the night from theirs. My mother has afternoon tea in the small square terrace off the room where she stays, and the terrace off our sitting room is where the dogs choose to lie in the late afternoon sunshine. Our most important terrace is the one where we gather as a family for meals. Situated off our kitchen, this walled courtyard is a mass of potted plants, small trees, creeping vines, and the occasional kitchen herb. An aviary stands protected beneath the outdoor staircase. It is home to our five lovebirds, handpicked by each of our five children. Around a long, well-worn wooden table we sit, arguing and jostling and feeling thankful.

By the time we built the Guesthouse and the Pavilion, we had learned the importance of porches and verandas. We decided that the money spent should mainly be concentrated on a nice house, of course, but that a generous veranda and really good mattresses also merited investment. After all, visitors spend most of their time on the beach, on the terrace, or in bed.

Recently the terraces of the Guesthouse needed some attention. We replaced the more obvious spindles with an X-form design nicked from one of David's clients. The new railings immediately changed the personality of the house, in much the same way that my mother's vision changed when she had her cataract removed. She says she went into the hospital wearing a brown skirt and came out wearing a purple one.

The architectural style that has developed throughout the Caribbean is clearly a result of the mishmash of cultures and influences that have wandered through. The French brought dormer windows, allowing the air to circulate freely, and hipped fish-scale tile roofs; the Spanish built cathedrals, churches, convents, and chapels. The Dutch had their detailed brickwork and cartouche-like gables, the Danes their neoclassical influence. And the English brought with them hints of manor houses and Georgian architecture, although greatly adapted for the tropical climate. So who brought the verandas and the porches? This will remain a mystery.

PAGE 118: The porch at King's Treat. Lovingly restored by David, King's Treat stands in a large walled garden with verandas that are shaded by palm trees and galleried terraces like this one, sheltered from the sun and the street by louvered panels. PAGES 120–121: The Guesthouse recently underwent a face-lift. Her balcony railings were updated from traditional spindles to a more elaborate X form. Took years off her. OPPOSITE: We deliberately left this space simple, as the light thrown through the wooden lattice above created its own pattern. ABOVE: Two views of the guest room terrace, known as Lady P.'s terrace, as my mother has spent many an afternoon taking refuge here, as evidenced by the bone-handled walking stick (right).

ABOVE: Two terrace seating areas and the much-trafficked outdoor stairs to our teenagers' room. The deliberate overhang hosts terra-cotta pots and young pineapples.
OPPOSITE: Kitty Soft Paws preparing for a catnap on the coverlet I designed as part of my HSN bedding collection. Following: Our main terrace, the heartbeat of Hibiscus Hill and the place where we think Mr. Friederich might be buried.

David & India
invite you to
join them in
celebrating their
18th
island New Year together
Hibiscus Hill
8:30 pm
31st December 2013
R.S.V.P. 333 2180

DRAMA

My grandparents were always entertaining, as were my parents, as am I. It must be in the blood. My grandmother in particular would graciously say, "Oh, do come and stay," to anyone of any interest, and then was faintly surprised when they actually showed up. As she was a woman of considerable wealth, endless people dropping by for endless parties never seemed to be a problem, although the Duke of Windsor arriving with Mrs. Simpson, who brought a cold chicken as a hostess gift, was somewhat confusing. But despite her wealth, my grandmother cared about certain frivolous expenses. When in the 1930s it became highly fashionable to serve a sponge cake alongside a good bit of dessert, my grandmother noticed after a few weeks of this custom that sometimes the cake would not be touched, so she sent orders to the butler not to cut the cake, but simply to offer it to guests and cut it only upon request. That way if it was untouched, they would be able to serve it again the following day. Both the butler and the rather grand pastry chef in the kitchen were horrified by her Ladyship's cost-cutting idea. On the copper-plated menu placed on the dining table the following day, the butler rechristened the sponge cake "*Gâteau d'hier*," or "Yesterday's Cake."

I find that living in the Bahamas rather encourages friends and family to stay, even without formal invitations. We've learnt that, like fish, guests tend to go off after a few days. So we built several houses in which to put them, but we invite them back across the garden for a meal every so often and always try to add a touch of drama to the occasion. That might mean lunch in our walled courtyard with the five lovebirds hopping across the tabletop, tea for two in the children's Wendy house, a surprising menu, a candlelit party on the beach, or simply moving our dining table to an unexpected place.

And drama may not always be provided by the setting. This past year, I realized David and I had celebrated eighteen New Years together. A cause for celebration, I thought, especially since we had skipped the getting married bit, so we have no anniversary to cling to. I assured Top Banana that we would be twenty, maybe twenty-five at the most. So she planned accordingly. And planning is essential when you live on a small island, as everything has to be flown or shipped in. But as anyone who has lived on a small island also knows,

numbers swell. A week before New Year, I plucked up the courage to tell Top Banana that the twenty-five guest thing, well, that had changed a teeny bit—we were now seventy.

This New Year celebration illustrates how David and I like to entertain. We always want to include our children and everyone else's as much as possible. This is especially true now that the children are a bit older and don't necessarily stab anyone with the cutlery. First and foremost, a celebration should always be a family affair. And every one of the kids should help, in whatever way he or she can, in the setting up and, I am afraid, in the taking down. The upside to having so many children is that many hands make light work. And you need to think of the upsides, because five sets of school fees make you wonder what on earth you were thinking in the first place.

I had seen a picture on Pinterest. (Yes, I'm a huge fan—after a few silent weeks on a damp, out-of-season dot of an island, Pinterest makes the rest of the world tantalizingly vivid and close.) The picture showed a long table stretching down a garden with strings of light bulbs hanging overhead. Striking, but a picture many of us have seen before, so how to make it unique to us? And then it came to me: a long table stretching away, but what if it curled in the middle, just like our driveway? So that's where we ended up having dinner—on the driveway.

With our number now at seventy, we began to beg, borrow, and steal chairs from all over the island. Mainly matching, occasionally a variation. We rented folding tables from the church, and I carried two gigantic china fish platters in my hand luggage back from New York. "Anything to declare?" asked the customs officer after I landed on the island. "Nope," I said, as though it was perfectly normal to carry fish platters on planes in one's hand luggage.

Teenagers on ladders were stringing up the lights as the smaller kids on the grass screwed in the lightbulbs. A little bit of child labor is okay, isn't it? David directed: pointing, guiding, arranging.

Bahamians are very keen on plastic flowers. They never die, they don't need watering, and they come in lots of bright variations. I see their point, but having grown up in a romantic English garden myself I can't quite

face a plastic flower. And having had some success with a florist in Nassau who had created a funeral wreath for me once, I contacted them again to send the same flowers, just not in a wreath. Roses, hydrangeas, hyacinths, pinks, creams, whites. The day before our dinner, the florist called. He only had hydrangeas and only in white, but it was not a problem, as they were going to spray the flowers blue. Sprayed blue hydrangeas? I nearly fainted.

Catering for seventy instead of twenty meant our served dinner was redesigned as a seated buffet dinner. It meant borrowing the fridge at the school and arranging for two extra pairs of hands in the kitchen. It meant my complete sets of white china now had to mingle with different breeds. It meant the muslin table runners ran out and we improvised with local flour sacks.

Although we could solve most of the challenges of hosting such an event with limited resources, the two things we could not do were to move the location or control the weather. By late afternoon, just as I had persuaded Nathan Turner and Eric Hughes to arrange hydrangeas (no blue, only white), it began to rain. All hands on deck, we dragged an old hurricane tarp from storage and rolled it out, with some insane, panicked idea of heaving it up over our seventy place settings. Just then the rain stopped.

But there was no plan B. I simply sent an e-mail to all our friends and family: "Bring brolly, looks like rain."

We were blessed, however, and the rain stayed away. In its place was a warm Bahamian evening filled with candlelight, laughter, close friends, family, and fireworks. Oh, and one very pretty, young, enchanting wife of a friend who began celebrating a bit too early. By the end of dinner—and well before the clock struck twelve—her words were slurring heavily. David, sitting to one side of her, leant across to Pavlos, Crown Prince of Greece, on the other side and asked, "Is that Danish she's now speaking?" Pavlos shook his head and said, "I speak Danish. That's not Danish!"

PAGE 128: The invitation I handwrote. A charming idea, I thought. And then it dawned on me there would be about forty more of these to write. PAGES 130–131: Wanting something a little more extraordinary than a straight long table, I decided dinner should be served on our curving driveway. PAGE 133: The monument David designed stood at attention all evening behind the small bar. Beware, small bare lightbulbs take forever to screw in. PAGE 134: I also hand-lettered the seating cards, which did not take too long, but the pressing and drying of the tiny petal on top of each card certainly did. Never to be repeated. ABOVE: There was quite a breeze blowing that New Year's Eve, which meant the candelabras did not behave, but someone arranged for the rain to stop, so I was not complaining. OPPOSITE: A generous but nutty guest brought a vast box of fireworks, handed it over to my elder children, and asked them to put on a show. They did, and remarkably the house did not burn down.

DREAMS

I dreamed of giving birth on our sleepy island with the crickets chirping and the palm trees swaying outside the small pink clinic. And then I woke up. The doctor was never there because he also looked after two neighboring islands, and the brand-new X-ray machine remained brand-new as no one was qualified to operate it. So instead I squeezed myself and my belly onto a tiny charter plane and flew to Miami with David and our potcake (mongrel) dog. In Miami, we bought the simplest of cribs. There were no frills to it, no bells and whistles, because we were probably only doing this once. That crib was used for fifteen years.

Many of the decorating ideas we had for our children's rooms were based around that crib. Simple wood with an oak finish. Fake, of course. For Felix, our first and therefore most indulged, David took the time to hand-paint nautical flags on the walls so that they appeared to hang around the room. The crib stood front and center with an inherited armchair upholstered in cornflower blue. When Amory followed in surprisingly quick succession, Felix was moved into the room above, where he slept in a big bed that we draped with a homemade Napoleonic canopy sort of thing in an attempt to make the move seem like an upgrade, rather than an eviction.

When Conrad was on the way, I knew he was a girl. So I painted the room white, removing any trace of the former flags, hung big framed black-and-white family photographs, and re-covered the small armchair in a neutral beige color. We aimed to make it not too girly, which was lucky, since Conrad turned out to be a boy. A fourth pregnancy resulted in a girl, named Domino after the James Bond girl in *Thunderball*, the 007 film set in the Bahamas.

Felix moved, yet again, from the biggest to the smallest room. In compensation, his two annoying younger brothers were not allowed to trespass there. Finally, he had somewhere he could be alone. The nautical flags returned, although this time they were not painted versions, but canvas theatrical props that David discovered in an antiques store on Nantucket. The two middle chaps slept in a pair of wooden beds with palm trees on their eight corners. A gigantic British flag was framed and hung on the wall between the beds, and Union Jack sheets were a constant reminder of the larger island where we originated.

Domino's room was painted ice pink, a color that carried a bit of sophistication with it. A series of 1790 red coral prints were hung on the walls, and the armchair once again underwent a makeover, this time resurfacing in a fabric of pale blue background with pink roses. Very English indeed. Once Domino could walk,

PAGE 138: The simplicity of this scene says so much. The dancer in her frame, the Union Jack ottoman, and the gilt-edged Louis XV chair, reupholstered in Sunbrella fabric to stand the test of wet bikini bottoms. ABOVE: My bedroom desk (left) and on the terrace beyond (right) a Peter Dunham cushion. I've known Peter since I was ten years old, and that was a long time ago, believe me. OPPOSITE: The paisley fabric I created with HSN sweeps our Cuban tiles. These were hidden under a thick white carpet when we first moved in. I can only imagine the previous owner must have longed for a home in Palm Beach.

OPPOSITE: We were very pleased with ourselves when we discovered palm-tree beds in an antiques shop. Admittedly, we are not entirely sure the bedposts are meant to look like palm trees. ABOVE: In case the children forget the other island, the one their parents are from, this framed flag dominates one of their rooms. FOLLOWING: A traditional sleigh bed against fire-engine-red graffiti-covered walls. Killer look or what? I try to remain positive about the kids expressing themselves decoratively.

Domino's room, where I still have a teeny bit of control. After four boys, we celebrated with a pink bedroom, which she no longer likes. OPPOSITE: My blue Paradise Toile quilt is a compromise. ABOVE: Coral prints dating to 1790 and a dusty rose armchair are hidden in the corner of Domino's room as part of her newly launched campaign against girly stuff. For those who don't indulge in AC, louvered shutters are still an important part of island life.

we decided the crib finally had to retire. A chapter of our lives was closing. The crib was replaced with an inviting wood-frame Swedish single bed with a pale greeny-gray (I am sure there is a more designer-y name for that color) head and footboard. It's a bed she can grow into.

By now Wesley, our beloved foster son, was with us permanently. The day after his mother was buried, he arrived at Hibiscus Hill carrying a bin liner filled with his worldly possessions. It was a very dark time. He shivered with fear at night in our guest room as I held him and tried to assure him I would never let go. It was Conrad, my youngest chap, who pointed out my mistake. Staying in the guest room, Wesley felt just that—a guest. I needed to move him into Felix's room. They had been best friends since birth, and now they were to become brothers. Felix did not hesitate, and Wesley moved in.

Not only do we now have five children, but we have three dogs, two cats, five lovebirds, and a tortoise. David says that is enough. That's forty-eight legs wandering around.

With that in mind, our own bedroom in Hibiscus Hill is our sanctuary. Okay, admittedly once in a while there is an extra body in our bed, be it a cat or a child, but on the whole we are fairly fierce about maintaining some privacy.

I spotted our bed in a design magazine. It was called the Lord Mountbatten tester bed. The company that makes it romantically names some of its pieces after Viceroys of India. Breathless with excitement, I called the company and explained that I was Lord Mountbatten's granddaughter, named after the great country of India itself, and that I lived in the tropics. The bed would also get photographed quite a bit. They were not in the least bit interested. Undeterred, I asked to speak to the owner of the furniture company. They would not put me through. By now they were convinced I was a lunatic. A few weeks later, I was at a design convention in Miami. I attended an evening cocktail reception, by invitation only, that was held in a building full of designer showrooms. Guests wandered from one showroom to the next, drinking, chatting, admiring, drinking. Guess which bed I spotted in one of the showroom windows? I went straight in and asked a nice, unsuspecting salesperson to point out the owner in the crowd. The rest is history, although the arrangement we came to was not nearly as pretty as the bed itself. Never negotiate with a cocktail glass in hand.

The most important thing about a bedroom is that it is a bedroom and should be all about sleep, and since we spend one third of our lives in bed (that statistic is definitely incorrect in the case of Banger, our dachshund, as he spends most of his life in bed), make damn sure you are sleeping in the bed of your dreams.

PAGES 150–151: All the four-poster beds in our guesthouse were designed by David and handmade by local carpenters, then completed with bloody good mattresses and bedding designed by me. OPPOSITE: Who doesn't want to sleep on top of, or under, John Robshaw? His fabrics make very suitable bedding for the simple, uncomplicated David Hicks bedrooms at Savannah. ABOVE: One of my rather brilliant brother's fabrics from David Hicks by Ashley Hicks is used as a highlight in two different bedrooms on two different islands. The finial on the top of the chair was snapped off by an unruly child.

ABOVE: A coconut husk–patterned quilt on top of chambray sheets from my HSN collection with my favorite beetle stitched in silver thread onto a coarse cloth cushion. As tempted as we were to redesign this inherited guest room, we decided that moving walls and upscaling the room would in some way diminish its understated island charm. And charm is an island quality we must never compromise.

ABOVE: Our own room, and the infamous Lord Mountbatten tester bed, in a sea of my paisley-print fabric, enjoyed by Banger, and on another occasion by Heidi Klum, who lay on it in her underwear during a Victoria's Secret shoot. I failed to mention this to David as it was taking place. He never forgave me. FOLLOWING: Several Hickses in bed together. An original David Hicks chevron cushion against India Hicks hemstitch sheets in front of a headboard upholstered in David Hicks by Ashley Hicks Herbert's Carnation.

ABOVE: I was going to make absolute certain the incorrectly sized sofa I mistakenly ordered at least made it into this book. No other reason for it being in here than that.
OPPOSITE: The ubiquitous Kitty Soft Paws claims the swinging chair.

STUFF

Stuff. Collections of it. How did we manage to accumulate so much? Hibiscus Hill is brimming with treasured artwork, children's pottery, travel tokens, artifacts gathered over the years. Every corner bears evidence of our fascination with stuff: always in a constant state of movement and endlessly reimagined.

My father believed one mediocre object on its own becomes something of interest when joined by others to form a collection. We apply this view to almost everything in our home. One orange in a bowl is boring, but a pile of oranges becomes a decorative statement. Michael Smith placed obelisks of lemons all over the White House, and Thierry Despont cobbles together menageries of bizarre creatures from old machine parts and farm tools.

Shells constantly work their way into our home. When carried back from dive trips and beach picnics by small hands, even the ugliest lumps of disfigured and disregarded coral are looked upon as treasure. These are added to an imposing mound now assembled on an upstairs terrace. The prettier shells and nuggets of coral are upgraded from the outside to the inside, finding a home amongst others in a wooden salad bowl or cubicle display case. Of course, I allow Domino, my youngest child, to feel she controls this vetting process, just as she feels she has decorated the Christmas tree, but as soon as she is asleep I steal back and reposition every ornament.

David and I simply don't seem to be able to hang just one piece of art; it has to be a collection. We begin with good intentions. A clean look, we think, and then slowly, slowly other things arrive, and we can't resist. One gilt frame leads to another and another. And why hang one black-and-white photograph when you can hang four more below it? In fact, why not create an entire gallery?

When playing around with piles of shells or lines of photographs or collections of any kind, I like to build them up and out as much as possible. Give them a bit of meat, so to speak. I also like to have fun with a collection by adding in something unexpected. Our shells live in an oversized wooden salad bowl, for instance, and others were glued by my own fair hand into the mismatched type cases of a printer's tray that originally held the different letters of the alphabet. Over the years, we have amassed an impressive assortment of straw hats abandoned by various people: fickle children whose tastes changed, guests who discarded holiday hats before their return journeys, even us in our own pursuit of the perfect Panama. This has led us to what David terms "the lending library." Guests borrow from this collection, which is housed poetically amongst our books and not, as you might have imagined, on pegs in the hallway.

I have kept scrapbooks since I was in my twenties. In them I preserve invitations, occasional press clippings, love letters, photographs, and other memorabilia. Presently in my forties, I have more than thirty of these navy blue leather-bound books. With strength in numbers, they now make sense as a collection and stand proudly in my office on shelves I had made to measure in order to house them. Each of my children creeps up the stairs (my office carries an R rating—you have to be over eighteen years old with a photo ID to gain entry) to find the scrapbook with his or her name on the spine, then steals away with it to spend hours with siblings arguing about who was the ugliest baby.

Our children are certainly collectors of stuff. My eldest son has persuaded me that one baseball cap makes no sense. What makes it valuable, in his teenage mind, is that it is part of a collection. A collection of caps. I know, I know—I fell for it. And Domino? All those Barbies naked in a basket document the stream of past birthdays. Amory has a collection of knives, and not just penknives, but big ones, too—cutlasses, Japanese fighting foils, his grandfather's ceremonial sword. They're all alarmingly dangerous, all requiring close supervision when handled, and all very beautiful when displayed together.

We built a new house for the overflow of friends and family, the Cricket Pavilion, inspired by a derelict building we stumbled upon hidden in the matted wild bush of Eleuthera. A swarm of slightly threatening bats was living inside this crumbling colonial memory. We thought this house would play in concert to our four-bedroom Guesthouse as they face each other across the garden, architecturally in tune with one another

from their exteriors, but singing quite different songs in their interiors. Both houses were intended to look as though they had always been there, built in a plantation style befitting the geography of their location. We positioned these houses to face north and south, rather than the traditional west or east. This way, guests had the chance to witness the fantastic light changing over both the bay and the Atlantic as the sun set and rose. Our Cricket Pavilion was named such as we built it in front of the track where my boys would bat balls back and forth along their imaginary cricket crease, wickets at either end. That house was going to be our minimalist expression. We intended it to be open and clean, painted completely in white. High ceilings, one grand room, a loftlike approach. We placed a circular table in the center of the room under the cupola that allowed natural light to stream down, and we set a simple display case with a few cupboards underneath to complete the idea. And then we thought the display cases looked empty, so we added two orange ceramic ginger jars. And then we thought our collection of distinctive Hermès gift boxes would complement the jars. And then and then and then. That was as minimal as we could be.

I was seven years old when I asked my father to write in my little autograph book. "Good taste and design are by no means dependent upon money," he flamboyantly wrote. I had absolutely no idea what that meant at the time, but now I think of his words almost daily. Nicky Haslam says the same. He told me he never buys anything for its monetary value. Instead, he likes possessions that smile back at him. Emboldened by these statements, I hardly ever buy anything for it's worth. Sometimes I choose something simply because it's unusual or unexpected, like our shark jaw, encountered by David in a market in Africa. Such was its staggering size that it put our local Harbour Island nurse sharks into perspective. We knew we needed to bring it home. Our bags stink of rotting flesh to this day.

I recognize that David and I suffer from compulsive collecting, but it's these collections of stuff that remind me of the wonderful times, the rough patches, and all those bits in between.

PAGE 160: Tom Munro photographs hang above a not-very-good antique chair recovered in Hicks' Hexagon. PAGE 163: This was only the faintest hint of what was to come. The entire room is now covered in hats, catalogued not by color but by designer. PAGE 164: David says this is simply a dust trap. He is correct, as always. But it also exhibits the shells I have collected over the years on diving excursions around the world. PAGES 166–167: We built our Cricket Pavilion based on the classical English architecture of the islands and an old clubhouse that we found hidden away in the south of Eleuthera. ABOVE: Our attempt at a minimalist loft approach. If we had been a bit more disciplined, the kitchen cabinets would have been omitted, but then where do you hide all the stuff? OPPOSITE: My father's abstract oil painting of Britwell Hill—a reminder of "England's green and pleasant land"—feels quite at home here.

OPPOSITE: A white birdcage we found at a Florida flea market—for once, I did not try to smuggle it through customs in my hand luggage. ABOVE: The pavilion cabinets, which we intended to hold nothing, have slowly been filled in our failed attempt to remain minimalist.

ABOVE: Our globe (left) and leather-cased telescope (right), which we sometimes use to spy into neighboring properties. Once a well-known movie star came for a drink armed with his own binoculars for exactly that reason. David and he went out into our garden, stood side by side, and spied into the garden next door. OPPOSITE: Felix's beautiful pencil drawing of a Roman bust sits amongst Domino's gallery of butterflies and hearts. All works of art and deserving to be framed.

OPPOSITE: This grumpy sod watches over the constant flow of friends and family staying in the Cricket Pavilion. ABOVE: All four of these vignettes demonstrate our compulsive desire to collect stuff. (Do notice those happy chic Jonathan Adler Ping-Pong paddle covers.) FOLLOWING: My father said hanging photographs on the wall was "terribly common." I always wonder whether that counts if they are just leaning against it.

175

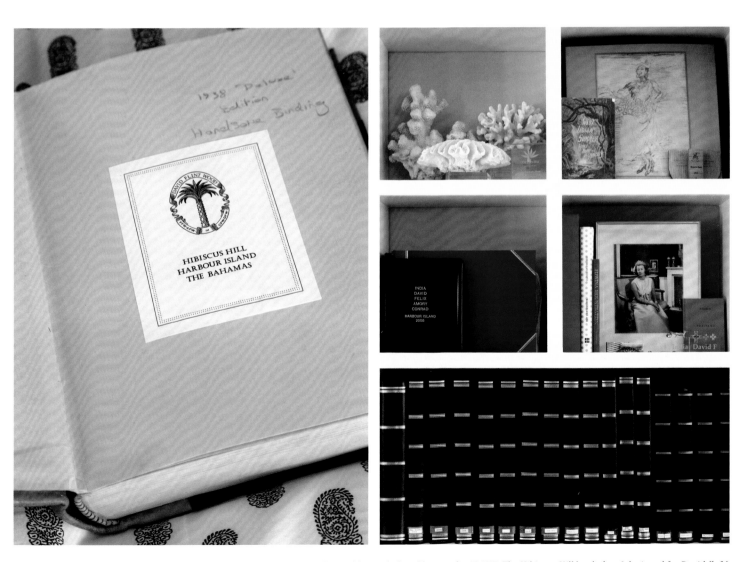

OPPOSITE: David's collection of shirts. They are not all his. Some were inherited from a beloved late uncle. ABOVE: The Hibiscus Hill bookplate I designed for David (left) and the shelves in my office (right) designed specifically to hold my scrapbook collection.

ABOVE: Each of these hats tells a story or two, especially when you consider that several have been passed down from child to child. OPPOSITE: Amory's rather impressive collection of knives. Don't panic, the big boy on the far left is light as a feather and made from plastic. But they look good together. FOLLOWING: Going with my father's theory that when one thing is joined by others of a similar nature, you have something of interest, I have saved these envelopes over the years.

Miss India Hicks
The Grove
Brightwell Baldwin
Watlington   O X49 5PF
Oxon

Harbour Island
The Bahamas

Miss India Hicks,
The Grove,
Upperton,
Brightwell Baldwin,
Oxfordshire
OX49 5PF

Lord Chamberlain
BUCKINGHAM PALACE
Lord Chamberlain

Ms India Hicks
Hibiscus Hill
Harbor Island
Bahamas

postcodes
sting dates
ristmas at
yalmail.com

Mr. David Flint-Wood
Upperton
ll Baldwin
lington
5 P F

r David Flintwood & Miss India Hicks

cks &
t Wood
ldwin

Miss India Hicks and
David Flint-Wood
Hibiscus Hill

NEW YORK NY
20 NOV 2009 PM

Mr. David Flintwood &
Ms. India Hicks
Hibiscus Hill, P.O. Box 255
Harbour Island, B-2000
Bahamas

00471+0001

CAP ADVISERS LIMITED
Dublin Branch
36 Fitzwilliam Place
Dublin 2 Ireland

Mr David Flintwood & Miss In
P.O.B. 255 Hibiscus Hill
Harbour Island
North Eleuthera
Bahamas

PRIORITY
AERPHOST

Mr. David Flintwood
and Miss India Hicks

Mr David Flintwood & Miss India H

Harbour Island B-2000
Bahamas

India Hicks
c/o The Lady Pamela Hicks
The Grove
Brightwell Baldwin
Watlington OXON
OX 49 5PF

BY AIR MAIL
par avion
Royal Mail

Mrs. David Flintwood-Hicks
Hibiscus Hill
P.O. Box 255
Harbour Island
Bahamas

PARIS 9. CHORON
PARIS NORD
20-12-07
882 00 022858
7956 752920
€ RF
LA POSTE
000,85
HP 126950

Mr David Flint Wood
and Mrs India Hicks
Hibiscus Hill
Harbour Island
The Bahamas

ER
BUCKINGHAM PALACE
03.10.08
SW1A 1AA

ROYAL MAIL
1
POSTAGE PAID GB
W7047

Miss India Hicks
% Lady Pamela Hicks
The Grove
Upperton
Brightwell Baldwin
Oxon OX49 5PF

E075
PBG 38927

Miss India Hicks
Mr David Flint Wo
The Grove
Brightwell Baldwin
Oxfordshire OX49 5F

NASHVILLE
JAN 19 20
USPS 37205

.80

Ms. India Hicks
Mr. David Flint Wood
Hibiscus Hill
Harbour Island

Mr David Flint Wood + Ms India Hicks
Hibiscus Hill
Harbour Island
Bahamas

REIMAGINED

I was helping my mother move from her London home. We unearthed box after box of handsome kidskin gloves, perfectly preserved in slightly faded tissue paper. Some short, some mid-arm-length, and some that trailed high above the elbow. Literally hundreds of them, in all different shades. Each glove had three tiny pearl buttons at the wrist, so the fingered part of the glove could be turned down when the bare hand was needed. Apparently this abundance of gloves was necessary during my mother's time as Lady-in-Waiting to the Queen.

I suggested we edit the hundreds down to a handful. "Oh no, darling, you never know which I might need and when." My mother was eighty-five when we had this conversation, and the gloves had not been worn since the 1950s. You have to admire her long-term view.

My father was the same—he hardly ever threw out anything. Instead, he would reimagine one thing completely into something else: his mother's dark red evening dress lining the wall above his library fireplace; an embroidered Nepalese shawl I brought back from my travels made into a pair of cushions; Italian marbled wrapping paper used to transform dull lampshades. Small clear plastic film canisters became vases for flowers; a terra-cotta flowerpot saucer was turned upside down, and my father placed an ormolu Directoire incense burner on top of it. He conjured new out of old and, in his inimitable way, contrasted rich objects with poor.

When we decorated a small hotel on Harbour Island on a nonexistent budget, we had to be very imaginative, from bringing piles of mosquito netting back from India ourselves to spending hours on our hands and knees sanding the floors. We designed four-poster beds that local carpenters could craft, thereby avoiding vast shipping and customs duties. Rather than purchase art, we delved into our Bahamian partners' archive of family photographs, which we then littered across rooms and public spaces, retaining the much wished for atmosphere of a private home rather than that of a public hotel. David designed a bar that seemed to have sprung from the pages of an Ernest Hemingway novel, and it was built, believe it or not, out of plywood, which we stained dark mahogany. Onto wood cast-offs from that bar, I hand-lettered the name of each room in gold paint then hung those signs on the bedroom doors to welcome the guests. We brought sand from the beach to fill the hurricane lamps, in order to keep the pillar candles from toppling over. The toile-patterned duvet set

that for years had covered me when I slept now possessed several tatty holes—cutting around them, the duvet became new covers for a stool and two chairs in one of the hotel bedrooms. We begged, borrowed, and virtually stole from Ralph Lauren, for whom I was modeling at the time, to acquire some good-looking rattan furniture, the embodiment of plantation style. And I lent the hotel two oil paintings of fat ladies that I had shipped out from England. My parents said I could have the portraits but not the gilt frames, which were evidently worth more. The carpenters were once again commissioned, and rather higgledy-piggledy frames were produced.

Shoestring decorating and the "repurposing" gene, inherited from my father, have stood me in good stead for island life well, the inventive side anyway. Without the luxury of department stores, fabric outlets, or decorating boutiques, repurposing becomes fundamental.

Not being able to entirely update our rather exhausted kitchen, I landed on the idea of painting the stainless steel kitchen chairs. Once a rather disgraceful amount of encrusted cereal and ketchup stains had been scrubbed off and three coats of high-gloss lipstick red had been applied, the kitchen smiled back in thanks, as did our accountant.

On the victory of this, I applied the same notion to our guest room. The room was flooded with morning and evening sunshine, but in the middle of the day it could feel a little gloomy. To brighten those hours, we had originally painted the room white. Now, two decades later, I wanted to change its personality in some way, without the bore and expense of a complete redecoration. Thankfully I had begun a collaboration with HSN, a home-shopping network that reached across America. Each year I created several collections of bedding, went live on television at ungodly hours, and told the audience that simply investing in a new comforter set would instantly update any bedroom. I went home and tried it myself. Our guest room had never looked so good. Simply by updating the bedding!

I moved on to the sitting room. After determining that the sofa, the anchor of the room, was what needed refreshing, I decided to look for something online. Unfortunately, I only seem to get around to Internet shopping late at night, once the office has slowed down. And I should admit the last time I shopped on the Internet

for one sofa, two turned up. Instead of putting two sets of covers in the shopping basket, apparently I had put in two sofas. (David was not happy.) And it's surprisingly hard to sell a five-seat sofa on a small Bahamian island. So this time I took extra care. I checked and double-checked that my basket contained one sofa and two sets of covers, and that is exactly what was delivered by boat several weeks later. While Top Banana was clearing the sofa through customs, she called the house and asked whether I had really meant to purchase a sofa meant to seat just two people. David did not speak to me for several weeks after that. Understandably. First two sofas and then another half the size it was intended. No longer allowed to order another sofa, the only remaining option was to re-cover our original one we'd inherited with the house.

We try to instill in our tribe of kids some sense of the importance of recycling: dog-food tins are stripped of labels and sprayed alarmingly jolly colors to hold pencils and paintbrushes. Wine crates store kids' homework; my mother's vintage hatbox is filled with valued collections of well-read magazines, and with happy licks of paint, the six-sided small wooden playhouse with miniature jalousie shutters and stable door has been reimagined for each child. Originally white, this "outpost of the Empire," as David christened it, has been red and white; all red; red, white, and blue; yellow; and now, dominated by our youngest, finally a girl, we went wild with pink stripes.

Many moons ago we were given a perfectly proportioned solid armchair. Perfectly proportioned, that is, if you were four years old. Each of my children has claimed this chair, reupholstered as each new occupant arrived, and enjoyed until his or her limbs could no longer fit, then passed to the next child. Samson, the golden-haired potcake dog we found abandoned on a neighboring island, also decided this chair was his when he arrived. As a small, terrified puppy, he would curl up here to feel safe, although in those first few months he could not figure out why the chair was shrinking under him.

Of course, every one of these reimagining examples is trumped by David Flint Wood's guest loo. Using our children's map of the world, he covered every inch of the walls. Making that toilet experience all the more global.

PAGE 184: Cecil Beaton's sketch of my grandmother beside a pineapple lamp and coral-colored Venetian glass fish, which are sitting on top of our children's bath toys. PAGES 186–187: David's chubby scrapbook, open to Arthur Elgort's photograph of my pineapple head. All the bits of scrap are kept in my mother's weathered hatbox. PAGE 189: A big old pile of India Hicks bedding, reinforcing my love of the island color palette and organic designs. PAGES 190–191: After two catastrophic sofa misorders, I was only allowed to update this forty-five-year-old one with new slipcovers. PAGES 192–193: Covering up. The kitchen chairs were painted watermelon red, and our nasty plastic water pump has a tailored rattan cover over it. PAGE 194: A fringed Bahamian flag bag, Junkanoo style—the brilliant idea of one long-established Harbour Island resident. ABOVE: How to update one room for kids of varied ages? A continuous battle of compromise. OPPOSITE: David's trump card—repurposing our children's map of the world into wallpaper. Everyone wants to use this loo.

OPPOSITE AND ABOVE: The Wendy house we built seventeen years ago has seen many residents, four boys and one girl.

ABOVE: This chair has also had many owners—five children, several cats, and Samson (left), who was outraged to find the chair shrinking under him as he grew from puppy to mature dog. OPPOSITE: Another flea-market find that I reupholstered myself using a staple gun and too much glue. My brother gave me just enough David Hicks fabric, but don't look at the back of the chair. FOLLOWING: Taking our "reimagined" theme into the garden, we updated a lost corner.

SILENCE

Silence. This is not something I hear a lot of. Probably my own fault. My grandfather called me Decibel because I was so noisy as a child. I had to be. I was the youngest of ten cousins. We grew up as one family, together every school holiday.

My grandfather was the backbone of our family. Winter holidays were spent at Broadlands, his estate in Hampshire, whose transformation into a stately Palladian home was begun by Capability Brown and completed by Henry Holland, two great names in British homes and gardens. Every Christmas Eve, we would hang our grandfather's thick woolen shooting socks on the mantel in my mother's room, never stopping to wonder how Father Christmas knew which of the numerous chimneys on offer in the house to climb down. In the summer we would invade his country house in Ireland. I'm not sure how it became known as Classiebawn Castle, as it's really not a castle, but a Victorian mansion with a tower. What is more surprising about Classiebawn is its commanding location—perched high on a promontory that juts into the fierce Donegal Bay. Many a happy summer was spent here, growing up wild amongst picnic hampers, lobster pots, and leprechauns. Classiebawn brings up darker memories, too. My brother and I were in the library there on a warm August day, watching Laurel and Hardy on the scratchy black-and-white television, when we heard an explosion. In the confusion and chaos that followed, we learned that the Irish Republican Army had planted a bomb on my grandfather's small fishing boat, murdering him, my cousin Nicholas, and the Irish boat boy, Paul, who helped out each year. My aunt, my uncle, and Nicholas's twin, Timothy, were taken to the hospital in critical condition. My uncle's mother—too old to survive the emotional impact of the bomb—died the following day. I was eleven years old, and I had never before heard of a political assassination.

I returned to boarding school just after the funerals. Although there was no moment of silence in the school of several hundred girls, I was relieved to be back in the dull routine of gray school life. And when I was overcome with grief, I would lock myself in the bathroom, away from the deafening noise of school.

Early chapters in adult family life were similar, although rather than grieving, at those times I was rejoicing in the gift of motherhood—but at the same time I was trying to survive the journey. With young children, the only moment of silence I could ever find was when I hid, locked in the bathroom again, away from the phone and the tribe of small people I had created. Absurdly, the master bathroom of Hibiscus Hill is the smallest bathroom in the house. One tiny sink, one squashed bathtub, one simple loo. We've always harbored a romantic dream of a room with a claw-foot tub, a sink for him and a sink for me, an armchair, and a view. It's never happened.

Before David and I built our offices, we camped out on makeshift desks in the old garage for several years. Regrettably rough concrete floors and bare shingled ceilings only seemed to attract our pesky children, until there were more crayons than contracts on those desks.

As our children and our professions grew, the need for privacy became increasingly urgent. Our son Amory, an honest chap, once answered a business call on my behalf and bluntly stated, "No, she says she doesn't want to talk to you."

So we removed the roof and built another story, two offices with a big conscious message that said: NO CHILDREN ALLOWED.

The offices were divided not only by doors, but also by our individual styles, which up to that point had had to be compromised. And who really likes to compromise?

David's office is lined with handsome dark-stained bookshelves that house his library of literature. The shelves are now so full that one has to navigate around towering piles of books that cover the floor to reach his 1860s Chinese black lacquer desk, which overflows with more books, on top of architects' drawings, auction

PAGE 204: A quiet moment, on a quiet dock. Time to breathe. PAGES 206–207: Classiebawn Castle, my grandfather's home in Ireland, where we would holiday every summer—ten grandchildren roaming wild amongst leprechauns and lobster pots. PAGE 209: David has all the characters and stories and adventures for a lifetime on a small island, right here in his office. PAGES 210–211: David's desk evokes Albert Einstein's question: "If a cluttered desk is a sign of a cluttered mind, of what, then, is an empty desk a sign?" OPPOSITE: My daily commute. ABOVE: Cupboards designed by my brother, Ashley Hicks, and artwork by our friend Anish Kapoor. Desk designed by me. It's somewhat impractical and normally has a cat or two asleep on top of the printer.

PAGES 214–215: The early morning light stretching out across our garden. ABOVE LEFT: Domino wandering home. ABOVE RIGHT: My five children, never predictable, always loved, perched on the roof of Hibiscus Hill. OPPOSITE: Our path to the beach. PAGE 220: Standing on my head, celebrating life. Pages 222–223: The beaches of the Bahamas belong to all of us. Entrusted to our keeping, to be looked after, and cherished, and handed on to the following generation.

house catalogues, tile samples, cigar boxes filled with pens and paintbrushes, ink bottles, and endless postcards, bought not with the intention of ever being sent, but meant to be looked at time and time again. It's not often you find David Flint Wood at his desk. There is no room.

My office houses all the high-tech things David refuses to allow to corrupt his. They are precisely laid out on a desk I designed, each piece of equipment in its place, polished and purring. Neat rows of sharpened pencils stand at attention. Even the paper clips are organized. I don't say this with pride. It's simply the burden of being a Virgo.

A pair of cupboards—designed by my brother—complete with slinky brass snake handles dominate the room. There are carnation pink walls and a small sofa upholstered in Peter Dunham's chocolate-and-cream toile. I cannot honestly claim that the room is a place of silence, but it certainly allows me to concentrate a little more on the business than on the personal.

For me, my time of silence comes as dawn breaks or evening descends on the three miles of pink sand beach at the bottom of our jungly path. Alone with my dogs and my thoughts, I run from one end to the other, catching my breath after the whirlwind of another day, watching the waves come in one by one, before setting off again for the unknown—no beginning, no end. For others, the hammock in our garden is a refuge and place of peace, perfect for a tired guest or sulking child. The pool, too, is tranquil in the late afternoon as the warmth of the day's sunshine beats off the flagstones and the hummingbirds suckle the hibiscus. Silent nights arrive, and all cries are hushed.

In those moments of silence I realize that my house is simply a series of rooms. What makes it a home are the memories, the objects, and, above all, my family. Without David and my five children I would have no home.

Having lived for close to two decades on this small island in the Bahamas does not make me an expert in island life, but when it comes to capturing the texture and distinct atmosphere that permeates island life, I think it might have helped. This book is about our own particular pattern of living, our creative rhythm, and negotiating our way through the noise and the silence of life.

ACKNOWLEDGMENTS

I would like to thank Jill Cohen for steering me in the right direction, Charles Miers for agreeing to it, and Kathleen Jayes for remaining calm throughout it.

To Sam Shahid for his discerning eye for design, and to Betty Eng who weathered the storm.

To my Godfather, quite a busy man, who took more than a moment to write the foreword.

To Linda Griffin, for running around, on more than one occassion, with a steamer in hand.

To Vince Klassen for his entertaining photography. To Colleen Duffley, who has the most generous of spirits and an ease with the camera, and Brittan Goetz, who for several years has photographed my children, my home, and my life with good humor and a magical understanding of island life.

Above all, though, a debt of thanks to Miguel Flores-Vianna, whose photography leads this book and sets the pace, and who always brings his old-world charm and good manners with him on his many travels.

This book would not be what it is without David and my five children. Without them there is nothing.

Claire Williams, our Top Banana, and Marissa Winder, who will always be part of our family.

First published in the United States of America in 2015 by Rizzoli International Publications, Inc.
300 Park Avenue South, New York, NY 10010   www.rizzoliusa.com

PHOTO CREDITS **MIGUEL FLORES VIANNA**: Pages: 36, 37, 38-39, 40 (left), 41, 50, 53, 54, 56, 57, 58, 59, 60, 61 (left), 62, 63, 64, 65, 66, 67, 68, 82, 92 (top), 93, 97, 98, 99, 100-101, 108, 116-117, 118, 120-121, 122, 123, 124 (top right, bottom), 138, 140-141, 142, 143, 144-145, 149, 150-151, 153 (right), 154, 155, 156-157, 160, 164, 168, 169, 170, 171, 172, 173, 174, 175, 176-177, 178, 179, 180, 181, 182-183, 184, 186-187, 190-191, 192-193, 196, 197, 200, 201, 202-203, 204, 209, 210-211, 212, 213, 216 (right), 224 **COLLEEN DUFFLEY**: Pages: 2, 6, 30, 31, 40 (right), 42, 44, 45, 46, 47, 48-49, 80-81, 87, 48 (bottom), 92 (bottom), 102, 104, 105, 113, 114, 115, 124 (top left), 125, 126-127, 147 (left), 152, 153 (left), 158, 159, 189, 194, 198, 199 **BRITTAN GOETZ**: Pages: 4-5, 22, 26-27, 28, 32-33, 35, 55, 61 (right), 71, 72, 73, 76-77, 86, 90, 110-111, 146, 147 (right), 166-167, 214-215, 217, 220, 222-223 **THE ESTATE OF DAVID HICKS**: Pages: 8, 10, 12, 14-15, 16, 17, 18-19 **INDIA HICKS**: Pages: 24-25, 74, 75, 88-89, 94-95, 106, 107, 128, 163, 206-207, 216 (left), 218-219 **VINCE KLASSEN**: Pages: 78, 83, 84-85, 130-131, 133, 134, 136, 137 **BRUCE WEBER**: Page: 21 © **LICHFIELD · GETTY IMAGES**: Page: 13

Design by SAM SHAHID

ISBN-13: 978-0-8478-4506-4
Library of Congress Catalog Control Number: 2014949600
2015 2016 2017 2018 / 10 9 8 7 6 5 4 3 2 1

Distributed in the U.S. trade by Random House, New York
PRINTED IN CHINA